Practical Careers in Computers & Technology Manual
Dawn Lucan

Introduction

Over the eighteen years that I have been an educator, I have been asked many times about selecting the right career for my abilities and interests. I know this is a difficult matter for someone who is disabled because I once faced this decision myself during high school. The best advice that I can give you in regards to this is that you have to consider the education required most of all. If the career requires a college degree, you have to take into consideration the coursework involved with it since college courses are more difficult depending on the major. There are some college majors that are very math or science intensive. I do mention if a college degree is required or not for the career. My best advice is to go with a career you love with the amount of education you can handle. Just remember that colleges and universities do offer help for disabled students including tutoring. Just remember when you love what you do for a living that life is a lot better for you. Good luck!

Dawn Lucan

Account Manager

If you love managing various situations along with helping others, you might want to become an account manager. You could be working in sales or providing a variety of different services to a company yourself. If you go into the computer field, you might want to get an associate's degree in it.

Animator

If you love to draw or paint, you might want to become an animator if you love using computers. Animators are artists who create stories being told on the television as a cartoon or animated movie theater screen. Most of these animated pieces are completed by computer. I recommend at least getting an associate's or bachelor's degree to enter into this field.

Automotive Technician

If you love cars and fixing things, you might want to become an auto or car mechanic. You could also fix trucks or buses. You could start your own business or work for a business. At minimum, you would need to attend technical high school, a technical school, or community college to get the training you need to enter into this business.

Bookkeeper

If you love math and computers, you might enjoy becoming a bookkeeper. You would be most likely working for small business. You would be keeping track of payroll, sales, but also invoices to be paid to outside vendors. You need a good eye for detail and deadlines in this career field. To enter into this field, some college to an associate's degree to enter into the field.

Brand Ambassador

If you love talking about a product or topic, you might want to become a brand ambassador. You would be representing a product in the store and having conversations with customers about it. The product could range from shift to shift or week to week depending on the needs of your company and its contracts. To enter into this career field, you would require a high school diploma.

College Instructor or Professor

If you love to teach people about technology or computers, you could become a college instructor or professor. They require you to get both a bachelor and master degree before hiring you. Your pay would be dependent on the pay scale at the college or university. The best part of them all is you would be preparing future generations for employment in technology or computer fields.

Computer Networking

Computer networking is a field when two or more computers work together within the same business or similar businesses. It can also happen at home. Depending on the business and job description, you would need at least an Associate's degree in Computer Networking or a Bachelor's degree in Information Technology.

Computer Programmer

If you love computer programming or helping people through computer programs, you could become a computer programmer. There are so many different fields in it as there are types of businesses out there. Fields include supermarkets, healthcare, financial, and more. Most businesses require a Bachelor of Science at least from a college or university.

Computer Repair

If you love fixing computers or things, you might enjoy a computer repair position. You could become self-employed or work through a company. You could fix a variety of different issues depending on your expertise and the business you work for. You can learn this career through your local technical high school, technical college, or community college.

Computer Security

If you enjoy the challenge of protecting a computer from hacker attacks, you would enjoy computer security. You would need an associate's degree minimum to start in the field.

Database Analyst

If you love mathematics and computers, you might want to become a database analyst. It is when you review the figures and make meaningful information statements about it in a report. Most businesses want you to have an associate's degree in mathematics, statistics, or economics. In addition, they may require some form of computer experience to get hired.

Digital or Computer Forensics

Do you love to problem solve and use computers? You might want to study computer forensics. You could work for the government or private industry. You would need at least have an associate's or bachelor's degree to enter into this career field.

Hospital Unit Clerk or Secretary

If you love helping people, you might want to become a hospital unit clerk or secretary. You would be transcribing doctor's orders on a patient for their medical file or even doing data entry. To enter into this field, you should have an associate's degree or technical diploma.

Installation Technician

If you love installing things, you might want to become an installation technician. This position does involve some travel associated with it in most cases. You could be installing a home security system, home entertainment system to even a family's computer system. This career field requires in most cases a high school diploma to enter into it.

Internet Marketing

Do you love promoting or marketing your favorite things besides surfing the internet? You could enter the field of internet marketing or promoting a web page. It can be done through search engine marketing or advertising on a website besides a newsletter. There is also search engine optimization. You can find books about this topic at your local library or bookstore. You can do this with a high school diploma if you go into business for yourself or an associate's degree if you want to work for someone else with their business.

Internet Sales Consultant

If you love handling questions from people, you would love becoming an internet sales consultant. You would help people get to know better about a product or service. It could involve making telephone calls. This career requires you to have at least a high school diploma and sales experience in the particular industry that you are interested in becoming an internet sales consultant.

Machine Operator or Manufacturing

If you love working with machines or tools, you might want to work in manufacturing. It is when you are working in a factory helping the company make the products found in our stores. You could be working with robots or not on the production line. You need a high school diploma, but most companies out there prefer you to be trained before hiring. You can find the training at your local community college, technical college, or technical school.

Patient Service Representative

If you love entering information into a computer and helping people, you might love becoming a patient service representative. Besides entering the data, you would be collecting copays from the patient or their family. You could be working at a local hospital, doctor's office, or other medical service provider. To enter into this career, you would need a high school diploma at least and customer service experience. However, there are some places that do require some additional training for their staff.

Robotic Engineer

If you love working with robots in a variety of different capacities, you would love becoming a robotic engineer. You would be working with robots in a variety of different workplace situations. This position requires at least an associate's degree in robot technology, electrical, mechanical or software engineering.

Robotics Technician

If you love robots along with fixing things, you would love to become a robotics technician. You could be installing, programming, or fixing robots in this career. This field requires at least an associate's degree in electrical or mechanics.

Sales

Within most companies and businesses, there is a department dedicated to sales. These positions can be located in your local community, store, or an office setting. Most of these positions are based on a commission or payment based on what they sell. For most of these positions, you only need a high school diploma and the ability to convince people to purchase the product.

Teacher

If you love working with kids or teens, you would love becoming a teacher. You would be working 180 days a year along with professional days as assigned to your contract. You could be teaching them about various aspects of computers. You would need a Bachelor's degree in education from a college or university along with teacher certification to start in this field, and some parts of the country require you to have a master's degree.

Technical Support

If you are good at computer software and solving problems, you could do technical support for a company. It can also involve computer hardware. This could be in person at a store, college or university, or over the telephone. This position could require as little as a high school diploma to a college degree depending on the employer.

Technical Writer

If you love to write and are good at explaining how things work, you might want to become a technical writer. A technical writer knows how to explain a complex technical matter in simple terms to help someone new to the software or game. You need to get a bachelor's degree from a college or university to get into this field.

Video Game Programmer

If you love to play video games and program computers, you would love a career in programming video games. As you know, the video game industry is a big industry with many new video games coming out every year. The idea comes from someone's imagination and what they believe someone might enjoy playing. It does take a lot of time to design and create a video game. For some simple video games, it may take a small amount of time but the more complex video games takes months to years to complete depending on how many video game programmers are involved in the process.

Video Game Tester

If you love playing games and good at diagnosing problems with computers or video games, you could become a video game tester. It does not require a college degree at all. It does involve problem solving to help the programmers discover the problems in the video game before it is released to the general public. This position does require being able to write out the glitch in the video game in enough detail to help the video game programmers to fix it.

Webmaster

If you love programming and have an artistic touch, you might want to become a webmaster. You can study this on your own because your local public library has books on how to create web pages, but you can also go to school for this. I have seen course offerings at the local technical high school for this, and I have seen my local community college. If you do this on your own, you could study on your own, but I do recommend you studying internet marketing including search engine optimization. If you study in school, you have a teacher and mentor who has experience in the field who can teach you the tricks of the trade. The choice is yours depending on the path you want to take.

Website Resources

www.careerbuilder.com
www.easterseals.org
www.fafsa.ed.gov
www.fastweb.com
www.indeed.com
www.monster.com
www.ncil.org
www.score.org
www.thearc.org